"Can Do"
Do"
Phonics

Sharon Clonts & Trudy Witham

To order additional copies of this book, contact:
Xlibris LLC
1-888-795-4274
www.Xlibris.com
Orders@Xlibris.com

This is

_____'s

Put child's photo here

Very own book.

Just get started
"Can Do" Phonics
Will do the rest.

"Can Do" Phonics has a number of varied approaches to stimulate the learning student as much as possible to aid in retaining the sound made by a letter.

1. **Sight** – Each picture cartoon has been designed with the specific purpose of aiding the beginning reader to identify the **sound** produced by each individual letter.
   - Look at the especially designed cartoon/picture together
   - Having your <u>positive</u> attention can be a great incentive.
   - Which letter you begin with is inconsequential – the important thing is diligence.

2. **Sound** –   Read each "Story" aloud a time or two and you will find that your Student will read *"Can Do"* Phonics by him or herself.
   - He/she should hear the sound of the letter repeated frequently.
   - Teach <u>ONLY the SOUND</u> made by the letter.
     a. At this point, the NAME of the letter is inconsequential, and unneeded to *Sound-Out* a word.
     b. AND in fact, merely adds to the uncertainty→"Is that squiggle the **sound** or name of the letter."
     c. For these reasons we plead: <u>DO NOT confuse a beginning reader by teaching the NAME of the letter too.</u>
     d. <u>PS</u>: [They will learn their alphabet soon enough! Again it serves no purpose at this point; and can confuse a beginning reader.]

3. **Physical activity** – In addition, each letter has an entertaining physical activity that will further aid in retaining the **sound** made by that letter.
   o Encourage your student to act out the physical activity that comes with each letter.
   o This serves two purposes at least:
      a. Applying phonics sounds becomes more fun.
      b. The activity becomes yet another stimulus to fix in the mind of the learner the **sound** made by the letter.

Encourage Don't Push

A. At each lesson, review before you move on to a new letter.
   1. Let the beginning reader set the pace.
      • Every child is unique and has differing natures and drives.
   2. Don't push – let it be fun!!
   3. Correct [when absolutely needed] VERY kindly!!!
   4. DO NOT CRITICIZE!!
A. DO!   Praise! Praise! Praise!
B. A little reward can be a great incentive!
   1. Praise is a terrific reward in itself but sometimes when your student has done especially well....
   1. OR reached a set target –For Example: When a child can say the sound of the letter without the picture to prompt.
   2. Since conscientious parents don't give out candy how about some little trinket from the 99 Store.

a - Sis has a monster and a goblin chasing her. What would you do? So does she! She yells - â - â - â - â - â!!!   [as in hat, can, mad]

- *Learning Activity: Pretend you have a monster or a goblin chasing you. Yell â - â - â - â - â!!! (as loud as Mommy [or teacher] allows.)*

a

b

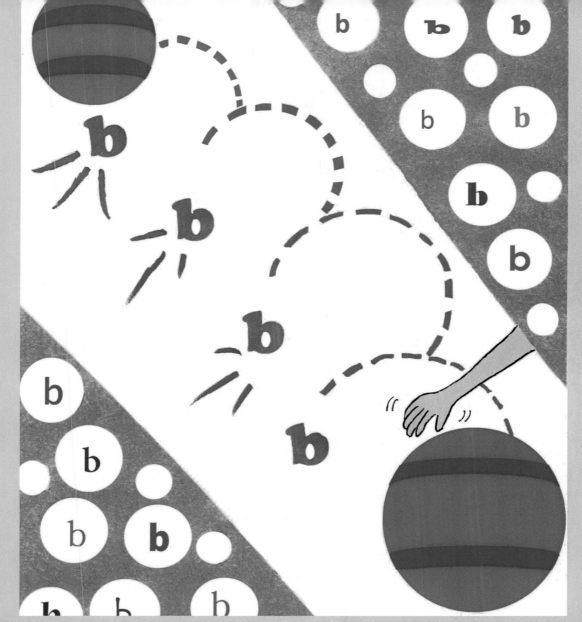

b - Do you like to bounce a ball? Have you evere noticed the sound the
ball makes as it hits the ground   b – b – b - b

- *Learning Activity: Bounce your ball…. Listen as the ball strikes the
  ground ……can you hear the b – b- b sound ?..*

C - Ret Betler c – c – c - coughs and coughs. As he coughs, his throat says   c – c – c   [Harsh "c" as in cat, cut, can]

- *Learning Activity: Hold your throat and cough like Jak c – c – c?   [Harsh C as in cat, cut, can].*

d - This is a magic drum; it plays itself - d – d – d – d – d – d – d!

- _Learning Activity:_ Beat on the drum. Do you hear?
  It says   d – d – d – d – d – d – d   doesn't it!

e - When Ben does not hear, he puts his hand to his ear to say - êh - êh - êh → ê - ê [as in êgg, fêll, lêt]

- *Learning Activity: Put your hand to your ear "I don't hear you" eh – eh → ê – ê – ê – ê – ê*

f

f – **What fun it is to chase a runaway balloon. You never seem to catch it. As it flits through the air you can hear it say f - f - f - f**

- *Learning Activity: If you have a balloon, get your Dad [or Adult] to blow it up but do not tie it up. Take your balloon outside and let it go. Listen....do you hear it..... as the air escapes the balloon it makes the f - f - f - f sound and causes the balloon to fly through the air.*

g - g - g - g - g

g - Hun must throw her head way back so she can g - g - g - g guzzle her drink.

- *Learning Activity:* *Throw your head back so you can gulp down your drink and speak* *g - g - g - g.*

ha – ha – ha – h – h – h - h

h - **Gotta laff, just gotta laff ha – ha – ha – h – h – h.**
There is the h – h – h – h sound.

- *Learning Activity: You can feel the laff coming, you try to stop it, but you can't here it comes ha – ha – ha – h – h – h!*
Can you hear the h – h – h sound?

i - **Look at the monkey at play. He scratches himself and goes**
î - î - î - î [as in sît, pîn, îs]

- *Learning Activity:* *Pretend you are a monkey? Curl your fingers around I the way a monkey does, hop around, Scratch yourself like a monkey and say î - î - î - î*

j - Beatnik Bug fell into a glass of ice and cannot get out.
Because he is very, very cold he shivers and shakes.
As his teeth chatter   j – j – j – j.

- *Learning Activity: You are just sooooooo cold. You hold yourself tight and your teeth "chatter", you cannot stop shaking and you say j – j – j – j.*

k - See the crow in the corn field. He is calling his bird friends to come and eat with him. You can hear him kaw – kaw – kaw k – k – k – k.

- *Learning Activity: Can you be a crow? Open your mouth as wide as you can – wider – now call your bird friends kaw – kaw – k – k – k – k – k! Did any birds come to you?*

I **- Jill sings opera in outer space la - la - la - I - I - I.**

- *Learning Activity:* *Here is your chance to sing opera!*
  See if you can throw out your arms, take a breath and sing like Jill
  la - la - I - I - I.

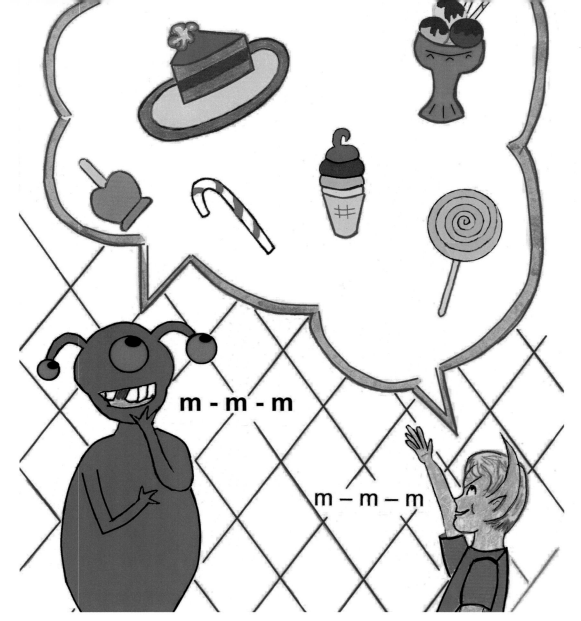

m - Ret and Ben are dreaming of candy, cake, cookies, ice cream. It looks so yummy - m - m - m - m.

- *Learning Activity: What do you say when you see a cake, or ice cream or cookies? m – m – m – m*

n

nnn-nn-n-no

n - **Pat is mad and bad. Nobody is going to tell her what to do!!!**
She'll show them!!! She'll throw a tantrum!! na - nu - na - nu - n - n - n!

- *Learning Activity: This activity is unusual fun. You get to throw a*
  tantrum! So do it! Stamp your foot [hard] and stick out your tongue to
  show you are mad. Now you say na - nu - na - nu - n - n - n!!!

O - Sam visits Doctor Cam, Doctor Cam says to Sam, "Open Wide!"
Sam opens his mouth wide and says? - ah - ah - → ô - ô - ô [as in
dôg, clôck, ôn]

- *Learning Activity: You are the patient seeing the Doctor. When the
doctor says open wider - open wide - ah - ah - ah → ô - ô - ô [short
ô as in hôt, pôt, môp]*

p

p - **Everyone loves popcorn. We all like to hear it pop. Do you know what sound popcorn makes when it pops? p - p - p - p**

- *Learning Activity: Clench your hands up tight in front of your face [palms outward] now let them out quickly as if they exploded [like popcorn]. Do that several times while saying the p - p - p - p sound*

q - Have you ever seen *A flock of ducks* Do you remember the sound
they make? Quack, quack all day long that is what ducks say|
- q - q - q - q

- *Learning Activity:* Flap your arms like a duck and say what a duck says
  q - q - q - q - q - q - q - q [not easy to say is it?] How do ducks do it?

r

r - Matt is flying over dinosaur country. He sees one, and the dinosaur sees him and roars at him rrr – rr – r – r – r

- *Learning Activity:* *Do you want to be a dinosaur chasing a space ship? You see Matt – he's the green alien in the space ship above – you growl -* → *rrr – rr – r – r – r.*

S - The "s" looks just like a snake and makes the same sound as well
s - s - s - s - s

- <u>Learning Activity:</u> *Can you make your arm curl up like a snake when you say s – s – s – s – s.*

S

t

t - Have you seen an old fashioned clock? The arm goes back and forth
– t – t – t – t – t

- *Learning Activity: Can you swing your arm from side to side like an old fashioned clock? Now, at the same time, make the sound of an old fashioned clock – t – t – t – t – t*

u - Look at that face! Dan ate all that green stuff now he is sooo sick - **uh - uh - uh → ûh - ûh - û - û** [as in nût, fûn, rûn]

- *Learning Activity: Pretend you have eaten too much and you are feeling just AWful. You open your mouth wide, stick out your tongue, hold your stomach and say* **uh - uh - u - u - u**

V - Racing space ships through space – va – va – v – v – v – v – v

- _Learning Activity:_ _You are in a race with another space ship. Now 'rev'_
  up your motor vvv – vv – v – v – v You're going to win vv– v – v – v – v!

wee-w-w-w

W - Sis and Ben are swinging - whee - whee w - w - w - w

- *Learning Activity: Pretend to swing back and forth, back and forth. whee – whee – w – w – w – w – w! We are swinging! What fun! whee – whee – w – w – w – w – w!*

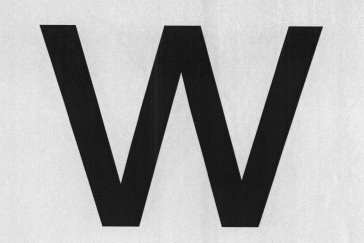

X - This is an X-Ray. It can see right through Pam [Girl Robot] to all her nuts and bolts inside   x – x – x

- *Learning Activity: Now this takes some real pretending. Can you pretend to see through your friend with your x-ray eyes? Do you see nuts and bolts or do you see bones and muscle, as you say it x – x – x – x – x ray.*

y - **Become a cheer girl yelling and cheering "yay" "yay" "yay" "yay"**
y - y - y - y - y.

- *Learning Activity: Get 2 dishrags from Mother or 2 wash cloths to use as your pretend pom-poms and yell [softly if you are in the house] yay - yay - y - y - y.*

Z

- z-zz-z

Z - **What kind of sound does a bee make?** z – z – z – z – z – z

- *Learning Activity: 1) You can be a bee circling around making the z – z – z – z – z – z sound.* OR
- *2) You can be watching and your finger can be the bee circling around while you make the z – z – z – z – z – z sound.*

It's

s - s - s - s

......The End

"I should have listened better to my intended while we were dating" He told me he wanted a large family. He mentioned something like "The 12 Tribes of Clonts" but more fool me, I thought he was kidding. When you combine his resolve with my familial heritage – you end up with a lot of boys. In our case it was 7 boys with 1 girl to give me strength to mother 7 boys.

My boys seemed to have a limitless amount of energy and so it became harder for some of them to concentrate in school. In trying to help, I began reading books about "How to Teach" etc. What I learned lead to my creating **"Can Do"** a Phonics to Reading Program. Each boy had varying needs or challenges, which brought about nips and tucks in our system. Our reward came in seeing our children's amazing progress in school.

Sharon Clonts

Trudy Witham

Trudy came into it, when her children received copies of **"Can Do"** Phonics and found that learning Phonics could be easy and fun.

Trudy lives in San Diego, California and has three children and 7 Grandchildren.

Trudy had her own very helpful input, plus she discovered a talent for editing. We gave out our phonics book to nieces and nephews and they found themselves ahead of their class in reading. Along came Grankids who naturally got their copy of **"Can Do"** Phonics Program, and they too found themselves not only ahead, but usually way ahead of their class in reading. So what with one thing and another, we have been able to test our Phonics→ Reading Program on over 100 children with unbelievable results.

Printed in the United States
By Bookmasters